AFRICAN AMERICAN ANSWER BOOK

SCIENCE
& DISCOVERY

AFRICAN AMERICAN ANSWER BOOK

SCIENCE & DISCOVERY

325 QUESTIONS

R. S. Rennert

Chelsea House Publishers
New York   Philadelphia

CHELSEA HOUSE PUBLISHERS
EDITORIAL DIRECTOR Richard Rennert
EXECUTIVE MANAGING EDITOR Karyn Gullen Browne
COPY CHIEF Robin James
PICTURE EDITOR Adrian G. Allen
ART DIRECTOR Robert Mitchell
MANUFACTURING DIRECTOR Gerald Levine
ASSISTANT ART DIRECTOR Joan Ferrigno

AFRICAN AMERICAN ANSWER BOOK
SERIES ORIGINATOR AND ADVISER Ken Butkus
ASSISTANT EDITOR Annie McDonnell
DESIGNER John Infantino
PICTURE RESEARCHER Sandy Jones

3   5   7   9   8   6   4

ISBN 0-7910-3207-8
ISBN 0-7910-3208-6 (pbk.)

PICTURE CREDITS
The Latimer-Norman Collection: p. 23; Library of Con-
gress: p. 42; Moorland-Spingarn Research Center, How-
ard University: p. 47; NASA: pp. 10, 15, 18; Nevada
Historical Society: p. 39; Schomburg Center for Re-
search in Black Culture, the New York Public Library,
Astor, Lenox and Tilden Foundations: pp. 26, 34;
UPI/Bettmann: p. 50.

CONTENTS

INTRODUCTION

In creating the BLACK AMERICANS OF ACHIEVEMENT series for Chelsea House Publishers, I was fortunate enough to work closely with Nathan Irvin Huggins, one of America's leading scholars in the field of black studies and director of the W. E. B. Du Bois Institute for Afro-American Research at Harvard University. His innumerable contributions to the books have not only helped to make BLACK AMERICANS OF ACHIEVEMENT an award-winning series, but his expressed commitment to inform readers about the rich heritage and accomplishments of African Americans has encouraged Chelsea House to draw from his work and develop the 325 questions that make up this *African American Answer Book.*

Each of these briskly challenging questions has been designed to stimulate thought and discussion about African American history. The answers highlight either the leading figures of black America or focus on previously unsung yet equally inspiring African American heroes, their achievements, and their legacies.

You can use these questions to test your own knowledge or to stump your friends. Either way, you will find that this *African American Answer Book*—like its companion volumes—is bound to educate as well as entertain.

—R. S. R.

QUESTIONS

1. What African American woman used the trial and error method to invent hair care products in 1905?

  a - *Madam C. J. Walker*
  b - *Harriet Tubman*
  c - *Mary Talbert*

2. Who is regarded as the father of sickle-cell anemia research?

  a - *Dr. Roland Scott*
  b - *Theodore K. Lawless*
  c - *Benjamin Banneker*

3. What was the name of the route, discovered by an African American frontiersman in the early 1850s, that helped pioneers and gold seekers travel to California?

  a - *Cumberland Gap*
  b - *Beckwourth Pass*
  c - *Sierra Madre Pass*

4. Who is a pioneer in tooth transplantation research and a graduate of Howard University?

  a - *Dr. Harold Fleming*
  b - *Jane C. Wright*
  c - *Sarah Garland Jones*

5. G. T. Sampson invented what popular home appliance in 1892?

  a - *Clothes dryer*
  b - *Electric stove*
  c - *Vacuum cleaner*

6. Who performed the world's first open-heart surgery?

    a - *Dr. Daniel Hale Williams*
    b - *Dr. Charles Drew*
    c - *Dr. Mae Jemison*

7. Who invented the shoe-lasting machine?

    a - *Jan E. Matzeliger*
    b - *Lewis Latimer*
    c - *Joseph Lee*

8. Paul Williams served as co-architect of what major international airport?

    a - *Los Angeles*
    b - *Chicago O'Hare*
    c - *Philadelphia*

9. Who was the first black physician in the United States?

    a - *James Derham*
    b - *Charles Drew*
    c - *Jane C. Wright*

10. Who invented the fire escape ladder?

    a - *J. T. Winters*
    b - *Benjamin Banneker*
    c - *Lloyd Hall*

11. Who was the first African American astronaut to fly in space?

    a - *Guion S. Bluford, Jr.*
    b - *Ronald McNair*
    c - *Frederick Gregory*

12. Who invented the pencil sharpener?

    a - *L. J. Love*
    b - *George Washington Carver*
    c - *Percy Julian*

13. What process was introduced by Dr. Meredith Gourdine?

    a - *Conversion of gas into electricity*
    b - *Modern way of making sugar*
    c - *Mass production of shoes*

14. Who invented the fountain pen in 1890?

    a - *W. B. Purvis*
    b - *James Forten, Sr.*
    c - *Frederick McKinley Jones*

15. George Washington Carver made paint and ink from what common food item?

    a - *Potatoes*
    b - *Milk*
    c - *Peanuts*

16. Who was the first female African American to enter the medical profession?

    a - *Susan McKinney*
    b - *Barbara Jordan*
    c - *Juanita E. Jackson*

17. Who invented the incubator?

    a - *Angela Davis*
    b - *Granville T. Woods*
    c - *Charles Drew*

18. (True or False) The electric stereo was invented by Lewis Howard Latimer.

19. What African American astronaut died in the 1986 space shuttle disaster?

    a - *Charles Bolden*
    b - *Guion Bluford, Jr.*
    c - *Ronald McNair*

20. (True or False) Norbert Rillieux invented the sugar refinery process.

21. (True or False) Lewis Temple designed a new whale harpoon that dramatically affected the whale-catching industry.

22. What home appliance did A. T. Carrington invent?

    a - *Dishwasher*
    b - *Refrigerator*
    c - *Range*

Ronald McNair, an astronaut who perished in a space shuttle explosion, accomplished much in his short life, earning a doctorate in physics from MIT, helping to develop new laser technology, and becoming a heroic role model.

23. Who invented the common dust mop?

    a - *Granville T. Woods*
    b - *T. W. Stewart*
    c - *James Forten, Sr.*

24. *Apollo 16* used an ultraviolet camera designed by what African American?

    a - *Ronald McNair*
    b - *George E. Carruthers*
    c - *Guion Bluford, Jr.*

25. The cash register was invented by what African American?

    a - *Lewis Temple*
    b - *F. A. Hilyer*
    c - *Louis Wright*

26. What position did Dr. Marchbanks hold in the first U.S. space mission?

   a - *Lead scientist*
   b - *Project physician*
   c - *Computer programmer*

27. Who invented the folding bed?

   a - *Andrew Beard*
   b - *L. C. Bailey*
   c - *Percy Julian*

28. The Holland Tunnel in New York City was designed and constructed by what African American?

   a - *Joseph L. Parker*
   b - *Ernest Everett Just*
   c - *Garrett A. Morgan*

29. Which of the following inventions was patented by an African American?

   a - *Jet propulsion balloon*
   b - *Telephone*
   c - *Cotton gin*

30. What scientist experimented with injections of vitamin C in cats and dogs in order to find a cure for epilepsy?

   a - *Harold Amos*
   b - *Wendell Belfield*
   c - *William Hinton*

31. Who invented the rotary engine?

   a - *Andrew Beard*
   b - *Lewis Latimer*
   c - *Garrett A. Morgan*

32. What African American woman invented fungicide?

   a - *Dorothy McClendon*
   b - *Dorothy Brown*
   c - *Ionia Rollin Whipper*

33. Who invented thermostatically controlled hair curlers?

   a - *Norbert Rillieux*
   b - *Solomon Harper*
   c - *Lewis Temple*

34. What system did Robert Shurney develop specifically for use aboard a Skylab space mission?

    a - *Computer system*
    b - *Waste management system*
    c - *Artificial gravity system*

35. What African American scientist recently discovered new information on how genes are linked together?

    a - *Dr. Robert Ratliff*
    b - *Charles Drew*
    c - *Percy Julian*

36. Who perfected a sail that helped larger ships glide through the waters easier?

    a - *Paul Cuffe*
    b - *Elijah McCoy*
    c - *James Forten, Sr.*

37. Who was the first man to discover the North Pole and to plant the American flag there?

    a - *Barney Ford*
    b - *James Beckwourth*
    c - *Matthew Henson*

38. The ironing board was invented by what African American woman?

    a - *Biddy Mason*
    b - *Sarah Boone*
    c - *Madam C. J. Walker*

39. Who was the director of the National Swine Flu Immunization Program?

    a - *Garrett A. Morgan*
    b - *Delano Meriwether*
    c - *Daniel Hale Williams*

40. Percy Lavon Julian played an important role in bringing what arthritis drug to the public?

    a - *Ibuprofen*
    b - *Cortisone*
    c - *L-dopa*

41. Who worked as an administrator for Freedmen's Hospital after the Civil War?

    a - *Harriet Tubman*
    b - *Sojourner Truth*
    c - *Frederick Douglass*

42. (True or False) Granville T. Woods designed the devices used for the underwater defense program of the United States.

43. (True or False) Elbert Robertson invented the mold used for making concrete pillars.

44. Charles Donaldson designed the sequence controller that was used for the landing system of what spacecraft?

    a - *Voyager*
    b - *Apollo*
    c - *The Space Shuttle*

45. Who was the first African American professor at Harvard University?

    a - *Nathan Irvin Huggins*
    b - *Dr. William Hinton*
    c - *Henry Louis Gates*

46. Myra Williams helped build space vehicles for moon landings during what decade?

    a - *1950s*
    b - *1960s*
    c - *1970s*

47. What famous dermatologist treated leprosy and syphilis?

    a - *Percy Julian*
    b - *Theodore K. Lawless*
    c - *Daniel Hale Williams*

48. Who invented the three-way traffic light?

    a - *Joseph Lee*
    b - *Garrett A. Morgan*
    c - *Lewis Latimer*

49. Meredith Gourdine invented what automobile device?

 a - *Battery*
 b - *Brake system*
 c - *Exhaust purification system*

50. Who performed the first surgical implantation of the automatic defibrillator in the human heart?

 a - *Edward B. Cross*
 b - *Dr. Levi Watkins, Jr.*
 c - *Frank S. Horne*

51. Who was the first African American to obtain a patent?

 a - *George Washington Carver*
 b - *Henry Blair*
 c - *Lloyd Augustus Hall*

52. What African American scientist is known for his work with insects?

 a - *Jan Matzeliger*
 b - *Charles Turner*
 c - *Louis Tompkins Wright*

53. Who invented the fire extinguisher?

 a - *Lloyd A. Hall*
 b - *J. T. Marshall*
 c - *Frederick McKinley Jones*

54. Who developed the first airborne radar system that was used for locating downed aircraft?

 a - *Ozzie Williams*
 b - *Daniel James, Jr.*
 c - *Guion Bluford, Jr.*

55. Who invented the smallpox vaccine?

 a - *Dr. Ernest Everett Just*
 b - *Dr. Louis Wright*
 c - *Dr. Lloyd A. Hall*

56. Who invented bullet-resistant Plexiglas™?

 a - *Lewis Temple*
 b - *James Forten, Sr.*
 c - *Emmanual L. Logan*

Highly skilled in chemical engineering and medicine, Mae Jemison became the United States's first African American female astronaut.

57. The Tidal Basin Bridge was built by what African American engineer?

      a - *Garrett A. Morgan*
      b - *Archie Alexander*
      c - *James Forten, Sr.*

58. Who invented the horse saddle?

      a - *Andrew Beard*
      b - *W. D. Davis*
      c - *Granville T. Woods*

59. What notable scientist, astronomer, and inventor was commissioned to help lay out Washington, D.C.?

      a - *Prince Hall*
      b - *George Washington Carver*
      c - *Benjamin Banneker*

60. What African American scientist received the honor of membership in the Royal Society of London?

    a - *George Washington Carver*
    b - *Granville T. Woods*
    c - *Benjamin Banneker*

61. (True or False) In 1913, Henry E. Baker uncovered 1,000 patents held by African Americans.

62. What physician introduced the intradermal method of vaccination?

    a - *Dr. Jane C. Wright*
    b - *Dr. Charles Drew*
    c - *Dr. Louis T. Wright*

63. Which of the following was not invented by Garrett A. Morgan?

    a - *Gas mask*
    b - *Traffic light*
    c - *Incandescent electric light*

64. Who invented a ticket-dispensing machine?

    a - *Frederick McKinley Jones*
    b - *Lewis Temple*
    c - *Andrew Beard*

65. Who invented a device for coupling railroad cars, which saved many lives?

    a - *Andrew J. Beard*
    b - *George Washington Carver*
    c - *Granville T. Woods*

66. Caroline Still Anderson was a prominent 19th-century:

    a - *Nurse*
    b - *Chemist*
    c - *Physician*

67. Who established a trading post that became the settlement of Pueblo, Colorado?

    a - *James Beckwourth*
    b - *Matthew Henson*
    c - *Madam C. J. Walker*

68. Who proved to be of great help in making friends with the Indians during Lewis and Clark's expedition into the Louisiana Territory?

   a - *George Bonza*
   b - *James Beckwourth*
   c - *York*

69. (True or False) Norbert Rillieux perfected a vacuum that revolutionized the sugar-refining industry.

70. Who became the only African American member of the famous "Edison Pioneers," Thomas Edison's collaborators?

   a - *Elijah McCoy*
   b - *Granville T. Woods*
   c - *Lewis Howard Latimer*

71. What did Granville T. Woods invent?

   a - *Telegraph system between moving trains*
   b - *Lubricating cup that fed oil to parts of a machine*
   c - *Incandescent electric light*

72. What did Lewis Latimer and Hiram S. Maxim invent?

   a - *A jet-propulsion balloon*
   b - *Railroad crossing switch*
   c - *Carbon filament in incandescent electric lights*

73. What did Andrew J. Beard invent?

   a - *Toggle harpoon*
   b - *Refrigeration unit*
   c - *Jenny coupler*

74. (True or False) Granville T. Woods was often referred to as "The Black Edison."

75. Percy L. Julian achieved his accomplishments in which profession?

   a - *Physicist*
   b - *Astronaut*
   c - *Soybean chemist*

76. (True or False) Garrett A. Morgan invented the first toggle harpoon.

In 1983, Guion Bluford, Jr., an aerospace engineer and astronaut, became the first African American in space. He also performed the first nighttime launch and landing in the history of the space shuttle program.

77. (True or False) Frederick McKinley Jones was the inventor of a refrigeration system for long-haul trucks.

78. Who invented a bread-crumbing machine and a bread-making machine?

    a - *Joseph Lee*
    b - *Jan Matzeliger*
    c - *Garrett A. Morgan*

79. Lewis Temple, the inventor of the toggle harpoon used by the whaling industry, was a:

    a - *Blacksmith*
    b - *Whaler*
    c - *Ship's captain*

80. (True or False) Joseph Lee invented a device for the railroad industry that helped save many lives.

81. (True or False) Dr. Lloyd A. Hall developed a salt formula to protect foods from spoiling.

82. (True or False) Lewis Latimer acted as a consultant in the construction of the first electric plants in the United States and Canada.

83. Who invented the device that made it easier to handle the sails of large ships?

> **a** - *James Forten, Sr.*
> **b** - *Norbert Rillieux*
> **c** - *Percy Julian*

84. Who invented the "third rail" track used by present-day subway trains?

> **a** - *Granville T. Woods*
> **b** - *Andrew Beard*
> **c** - *Jan Matzeliger*

85. (True or False) Jean Baptiste Pointe DuSable was the founder and first settler of Cleveland, Ohio.

86. Benjamin Montgomery invented a boat propeller in 1850. At the time, he was a slave owned by:

> **a** - *Robert E. Lee*
> **b** - *Jefferson Davis*
> **c** - *Stonewall Jackson*

87. What was the name of the first all-black medical school?

> **a** - *Howard University*
> **b** - *Fisk University*
> **c** - *Meharry Medical College*

88. Who discovered a passage through the Sierra Nevada in the early 1800s?

> **a** - *James Beckwourth*
> **b** - *Matthew Henson*
> **c** - *Paul Cuffe*

89. Why did Native Americans nickname James Beckwourth "Enemy of Horses"?

    a - *Because he tamed wild horses*
    b - *Because he stole horses from white men*
    c - *Because he was a champion rodeo rider*

90. Who corresponded with Thomas Jefferson, explaining both his scientific insights and his criticisms of slavery?

    a - *Paul Cuffe*
    b - *Benjamin Banneker*
    c - *Ernest Everett Just*

91. Joseph Lee's bread-making invention did the work of how many people each day?

    a - *Three*
    b - *Eight*
    c - *Twelve*

92. Where was George Washington Carver born into slavery?

    a - *Diamond Grove, Missouri*
    b - *Athens, Georgia*
    c - *Knoxville, Tennessee*

93. (True or False) George Washington Carver received a master's degree in agriculture.

94. In what year did George Washington Carver die?

    a - *1843*
    b - *1919*
    c - *1943*

95. Where is Meharry Medical College located?

    a - *Tennessee*
    b - *Alabama*
    c - *Georgia*

96. In what year was the first all-black medical school, Meharry Medical College, established?

    a - *1846*
    b - *1876*
    c - *1896*

97. What was the Indian name of Chicago at the time of Jean Baptiste Pointe DuSable's settlement?

    a - *Eschikagou*
    b - *Waukegan*
    c - *Tamaqua*

98. (True or False) Dr. Edward S. Cooper became the first African American president of the American Cancer Association.

99. Who became General John C. Fremont's chief scout in 1848?

    a - *James Beckwourth*
    b - *Barney Ford*
    c - *Jean DuSable*

100. In what city was Norbert Rillieux, inventor and scientist, born in 1806?

    a - *Washington, D.C.*
    b - *New Orleans, Louisiana*
    c - *Birmingham, Alabama*

101. What breakthrough medical procedure was performed by Dr. Daniel Hale Williams?

    a - *Open-heart surgery*
    b - *Blood transfusion*
    c - *Kidney transplant*

102. Which of the following inventions was patented by an African American?

    a - *Cotton gin*
    b - *Rotary engine*
    c - *Copy machine*

103. Which of the following inventions was patented by an African American?

    a - *Dishwasher*
    b - *Automobile*
    c - *Fertilizer distributor*

104. Zoologist Ernest Everett Just was known for his research on:

> **a** - *Marine eggs*
> **b** - *Poisonous sea creatures*
> **c** - *Aquatic plant life*

105. (True or False) Dr. Charles R. Drew was regarded as the "Father of Blood Plasma."

106. Commander Robert E. Peary reached the North Pole with what African American explorer?

> **a** - *Matthew Henson*
> **b** - *James Beckwourth*
> **c** - *Ronald McNair*

107. Who received a patent for the invention of an optical apparatus that helped to position tooling?

> **a** - *Granville T. Woods*
> **b** - *D. E. Howard*
> **c** - *Lewis Latimer*

108. What African American patented the corn harvester?

> **a** - *Benjamin Banneker*
> **b** - *James Forten, Sr.*
> **c** - *Henry T. Blair*

109. Estevanico (Little Stephen) was a black slave who participated in an exploration from Mexico into the U.S. and discovered what states?

> **a** - *California and Nevada*
> **b** - *Arizona and New Mexico*
> **c** - *Colorado and Utah*

110. (True or False) Matthew Henson is recognized as a co-discoverer of the Antarctic Circle.

111. Who is Matthew Henson buried next to in Arlington, Virginia?

> **a** - *James Beckwourth*
> **b** - *Admiral Robert E. Peary*
> **c** - *Frederick Cook*

A self-trained draftsman and brilliant inventor, Lewis Latimer revolutionized the field of electric lighting by inventing the inexpensive, long-lasting carbon filament for light bulbs.

112. What aerospace engineer was awarded 10 air force medals for competence and bravery during the Vietnam War?

     a - *Ronald McNair*
     b - *Charles Donaldson*
     c - *Guion Bluford, Jr.*

113. What inventor was instrumental in the development of automatic lubricators for machinery?

     a - *Elijah McCoy*
     b - *Lewis Latimer*
     c - *Benjamin Banneker*

114. Who patented a telephone transmitter that was bought by Bell Telephone?

    a - *Lewis Latimer*
    b - *Granville T. Woods*
    c - *Frederick McKinley Jones*

115. What African American was called in to assist a rescue effort for six workers trapped by a gas explosion using his patented smoke mask?

    a - *Garrett A. Morgan*
    b - *Lewis Latimer*
    c - *Benjamin Banneker*

116. Who was known as the "Black Apollo of Science"?

    a - *Ernest Everett Just*
    b - *George Washington Carver*
    c - *Charles Drew*

117. Who received the gold medal for "Distinguished Service in the Field of Chemistry"?

    a - *George Washington Carver*
    b - *Dolphus Milligan*
    c - *Lewis Latimer*

118. What African American explorer participated in an expedition through Nicaragua to discover a route for a canal linking the Atlantic and Pacific?

    a - *Matthew Henson*
    b - *Estevanico*
    c - *James Beckwourth*

119. Who invented a revolving brush used to clean streets?

    a - *Frederick McKinley Jones*
    b - *Jan Matzeliger*
    c - *Charles Brooks*

120. Who built the first American-made wooden clock?

    a - *Paul Cuffe*
    b - *Lewis Latimer*
    c - *Benjamin Banneker*

121. Who is famous for research on sickle-cell anemia?

    a - *Dr. Charles Drew*
    b - *Dr. Roland Scott*
    c - *Dr. Robert Ratliff*

122. Who received an award from the U.S. Army for developing techniques to decontaminate missiles?

    a - *Lewis Latimer*
    b - *Garrett A. Morgan*
    c - *Bruce Lee*

123. What pioneering African American nurse was thought to be the first black woman in Boston to register for the vote after the passage of the Nineteenth Amendment?

    a - *Harriet Tubman*
    b - *Mary Elizabeth Mahoney*
    c - *Justina Ford*

124. (True or False) Dorothy McClendon and Mary Lampkin are respected African American scientists.

125. Who invented the lawn sprinkler?

    a - *Norbert Rillieux*
    b - *J. W. Smith*
    c - *Lewis Temple*

126. Who patented the folding chair?

    a - *James Briscoe*
    b - *Charles Beckley*
    c - *Andrew Beard*

127. Who developed the largest research and training center for kidney transplants in the country?

    a - *Dr. Charles Drew*
    b - *Dr. Samuel L. Koontz*
    c - *Dr. Mae Jemison*

128. Who invented the lawn mower?

    a - *James Forten*
    b - *J. A. Burr*
    c - *Lewis Latimer*

Granville T. Woods earned more than 50 patents for his ingenious inventions, primarily in the areas of railroad telegraphs and electrical railway systems.

129. Who invented the mailbox?

> **a** - *E. G. Becket*
> **b** - *Frederick McKinley Jones*
> **c** - *Joseph Lee*

130. Who was the first woman assigned by the U.S. Navy to study underwater acoustics?

> **a** - *Mary Middleton*
> **b** - *Mae Jemison*
> **c** - *Maggie Lena Walker*

131. Who invented the burglar alarm?

    a - *Percy L. Julian*
    b - *Louis Alexander*
    c - *Andrew Beard*

132. Who predicted the eclipse of the sun in 1789?

    a - *Benjamin Banneker*
    b - *Richard Allen*
    c - *Prince Hall*

133. Who invented the control unit for the artificial heart stimulator?

    a - *Daniel Hale Williams*
    b - *Louis Wright*
    c - *Otis Boykin*

134. Who patented the envelope seal in 1897?

    a - *Lewis Latimer*
    b - *F. W. Leslie*
    c - *Lloyd A. Hall*

135. Who invented the technique of using dye to detect liver disease and to evaluate blood?

    a - *Dr. Charles Drew*
    b - *Dr. Carrol M. Leevy*
    c - *Ernest Everett Just*

136. Who invented the refrigerator?

    a - *J. Standard*
    b - *Elijah McCoy*
    c - *Granville T. Woods*

137. Who is responsible for perfecting the technique of preserving plasma for blood banks?

    a - *Dr. Charles Drew*
    b - *Dr. Louis Wright*
    c - *Dr. Percy Julian*

138. What African American developed a treatment for arthritis?

    a - *Dr. Percy Julian*
    b - *Dr. Jane C. Wright*
    c - *Dr. Charles Drew*

139. Who patented corrosion-resistant alloy steels?

    a - *James Parsons*
    b - *Lloyd Hall*
    c - *Percy Julian*

140. (True or False) Dr. Mae Jemison was the first African American female nuclear engineer.

141. Who invented the automatic gear shift?

    a - *Jan Matzeliger*
    b - *R. B. Spike*
    c - *Lewis Latimer*

142. Who designed and patented the dustpan?

    a - *James Forten, Sr.*
    b - *L. P. Ray*
    c - *Frederick McKinley Jones*

143. Who invented the fuel mixture for the Polaris missile?

    a - *Garrett A. Morgan*
    b - *Booker T. Hoagan*
    c - *Charles Drew*

144. Traffic lights were invented by:

    a - *Garrett A. Morgan*
    b - *Andrew Beard*
    c - *Frederick McKinley Jones*

145. Who developed an advanced method for determining the metal content of ore?

    a - *Joseph Lee*
    b - *Charles Drew*
    c - *Charles Spurgeon Fletcher*

146. Who invented portable refrigeration?

    a - *Frederick McKinley Jones*
    b - *Lewis Howard Latimer*
    c - *Granville T. Woods*

147. Who invented the door lock?

    a - *James Forten, Sr.*
    b - *A. W. Martin*
    c - *Joseph Lee*

148. Who developed the test used to detect the disease syphilis?

    a - *William Hinton*
    b - *Louis Wright*
    c - *Dr. Charles Drew*

149. Who invented the electron microscope?

    a - *John Coleman*
    b - *Elijah McCoy*
    c - *Norbert Rillieux*

150. Who led groundbreaking tests in the use of chemotherapy while director of the Harlem Hospital Cancer Research Foundation?

    a - *Dr. Austin Curtis*
    b - *Dr. Daniel Hale Williams*
    c - *Dr. Jane C. Wright*

151. What African American did research at the renowned Marine Biological Laboratory at Woods Hole, Massachusetts, in the early 1900s?

    a - *Dr. Charles Drew*
    b - *Ernest Everett Just*
    c - *George Washington Carver*

152. (True or False) Dr. Harold Fleming is well known for his research in tooth transplantation.

153. Who managed health care for the Peace Corps in Sierra Leone and Liberia in West Africa?

    a - *Dr. Mae Jemison*
    b - *Dr. Daniel Hale Williams*
    c - *Dr. Louis Wright*

154. In what year did Guion Bluford, Jr., become the first African American to journey into space?

    a - *1978*
    b - *1980*
    c - *1983*

155. Who is responsible for inventing the method of converting gas into electricity for everyday use?

    a - *Meredith Gourdine*
    b - *Jan Matzeliger*
    c - *Benjamin Banneker*

156. What black servant introduced inoculation against smallpox to the American colonies?

    a - *Benjamin Banneker*
    b - *Onesimus*
    c - *Estevanico*

157. What African American inventor lied about his age so that he could join the U.S. Navy and fight the South in the Civil War?

    a - *Lewis Latimer*
    b - *George Washington Carver*
    c - *Granville T. Woods*

158. What black scientist considered becoming a painter instead?

    a - *Benjamin Banneker*
    b - *George Washington Carver*
    c - *Ernest Everett Just*

159. (True or False) The Tuskegee Institute was founded by George Washington Carver in 1881.

160. Dr. Daniel Hale Williams performed the world's first open-heart surgery at what hospital?

    a - *Chicago's Provident Hospital*
    b - *Philadelphia's Jefferson Hospital*
    c - *Washington, D.C.'s Walter Reed Hospital*

161. (True or False) As a student at McGill University, Charles Drew became one of Canada's top track athletes.

162. (True or False) Dr. Charles Drew was the first African American physician to receive a municipal hospital position appointment in New York City.

163. In what year did Garrett A. Morgan invent the automatic traffic signal?

     a - *1923*
     b - *1933*
     c - *1899*

164. After Dr. Daniel Hale Williams performed the first successful open-heart surgery in 1893, how many more years did his patient live?

     a - *10*
     b - *15*
     c - *20*

165. Rebecca Lee Crumpler was the first accredited African American woman:

     a - *Physician*
     b - *Chemist*
     c - *Biologist*

166. Dr. James Derham was recognized in the 1790s as an outstanding specialist for what type of medical disorders?

     a - *Liver*
     b - *Kidney*
     c - *Throat*

167. Ronald McNair, Charles Bolden, and Frederick Gregory pursued what career?

     a - *Inventor*
     b - *Astronaut*
     c - *Biologist*

168. Who resigned as coordinator for the American Red Cross blood bank program because he disagreed with a directive from the War Department stating that blood from black donors should not be mixed with blood from white donors?

    a - *Percy Julian*
    b - *Charles Drew*
    c - *Roland Scott*

169. Whose refrigeration system completely changed the way food could be transported?

    a - *Frederick McKinley Jones*
    b - *Lewis Latimer*
    c - *Lewis Temple*

170. (True or False) Lloyd Hall revolutionized the meat-packing industry with his discovery of curing salts.

171. What kind of association was the Medico-Chirurgical Society, which was formed in 1884?

    a - *Black inventors association*
    b - *Black medical association*
    c - *Black pharmaceutical association*

172. (True or False) Jesse Leroy Brown was the first African American naval aviator.

173. What African American inventor received a patent for the elevator in 1887?

    a - *A. Miles*
    b - *Granville T. Woods*
    c - *Lewis Latimer*

174. Who made the first practical shoe-making machine that revolutionized the shoe industry?

    a - *George Washington Carver*
    b - *Lewis Latimer*
    c - *Jan Matzeliger*

175. What African American devised a way to prolong the life of plastic?

    a - *George Washington Carver*
    b - *Lewis Latimer*
    c - *W. Lincoln Hawkins*

176. In what year did Dr. Ida Gray become the first accredited African American female dentist?

  a - *1890*
  b - *1901*
  c - *1916*

177. Who saved the lives of thousands of soldiers in World War II with his invention of "aerofoam"?

  a - *Charles Drew*
  b - *Percy Julian*
  c - *Lewis Latimer*

178. Who developed a drug used to treat glaucoma, an eye disease?

  a - *Dr. Percy Julian*
  b - *Dr. Charles Drew*
  c - *Ernest Everett Just*

179. (True or False) Norbert Rillieux submitted a complex proposal for a sewer system to the city of New Orleans.

180. Who developed mathematical formulas to calculate weather and astronomical events?

  a - *Benjamin Banneker*
  b - *Shirley Ann Jackson*
  c - *Lewis Latimer*

181. What black slave helped Cyrus McCormick invent his famous reaper?

  a - *Joe Anderson*
  b - *Lewis Temple*
  c - *James Forten, Sr.*

182. When was Jean Baptiste Pointe DuSable officially recognized as the founder of Chicago?

  a - *1868*
  b - *1916*
  c - *1968*

183. What invention made James Forten, Sr., one of the wealthiest men in America?

  a - *Shoe-making machine*
  b - *Refrigeration system*
  c - *Sail control for ships*

America's first black man of science, Benjamin Banneker became a respected astronomer, mathematician, surveyor, and publisher of a popular almanac in the late 18th century.

184. Who was the first African American to win the NAACP Spingarn Medal?

    a - *Ernest Everett Just*
    b - *George Washington Carver*
    c - *Charles Drew*

185. Who prepared the blueprints for Alexander Graham Bell's telephone?

    a - *Lewis Latimer*
    b - *Jan Matzeliger*
    c - *George Washington Carver*

186. Who invented the oil stove and the refrigerator?

    a - *Asa Whirlpool*
    b - *J. Standard*
    c - *B. H. Amana*

187. Who reported that a black man came to her in a dream and gave her a secret formula for growing hair?

    a - *Julia Hammond*
    b - *Madam C. J. Walker*
    c - *Sojourner Truth*

188. Prior to Norbert Rillieux's invention, what was the name of the method used to refine sugarcane juice into granular sugar?

    a - *Jamaica Train*
    b - *Brown Boiler*
    c - *Sugar Boiler*

189. (True or False) George Washington Carver won the Spingarn Medal for his distinguished research of dairy cows' milk production.

190. Who was the first African American professionally trained as a registered nurse in the United States?

    a - *Mary Mahoney*
    b - *Harriet Tubman*
    c - *Mary McLeod Bethune*

191. Who became the first African American executive of a major airline company (Eastern)?

    a - *Benjamin O. Davis, Jr.*
    b - *James O. Plinton, Jr.*
    c - *Guion Bluford, Jr.*

192. What did J. F. Pickering patent in 1900?

    a - *Lawn mower*
    b - *Digital radio*
    c - *Modified airship*

193. After Eli Whitney invented the cotton gin, what kind of labor became more prevalent in the South?

    a - *Sharecropping*
    b - *Slave labor*
    c - *Industrial labor*

194. In 1872, what inventor received a patent for an apparatus for detaching horses from carriages?

    a - *T. J. Boyd*
    b - *Lewis Latimer*
    c - *Elijah McCoy*

195. Where was George Washington Carver's lab?

    a - *Tuskegee Institute, Alabama*
    b - *Lincoln University, Missouri*
    c - *Howard University, Washington, D.C.*

196. How much money did Garrett A. Morgan receive from General Electric for his automatic stop sign invention?

    a - *$5,000*
    b - *$20,000*
    c - *$40,000*

197. What biological scientist researched egg fertilization?

    a - *George Washington Carver*
    b - *Dr. Ernest Everett Just*
    c - *Dr. Charles Drew*

198. Norbert Rillieux's discovery of "multiple effect evaporation" helped in refining sugar and was also applied to:

    a - *Production of condensed milk*
    b - *Production of soap and glue*
    c - *Both a and b*

199. What was the significance of the 10th Cavalry in the Old West?

    a - *First integrated cavalry*
    b - *All-black cavalry*
    c - *Fought at "Custer's Last Stand"*

200. What was the nature of the work that scientist J. Ernest Wilkins, Jr., did on the "Manhattan Project"?

    a - *Develop atomic power*
    b - *Develop electric power*
    c - *Develop spy technology*

201. Who was regarded as the savior of southern agriculture?

    a - *Ernest Everett Just*
    b - *George Washington Carver*
    c - *Elijah McCoy*

202. What African American politician worked as a chemist before entering law school?

    a - *Jesse Jackson*
    b - *L. Douglas Wilder*
    c - *David Dinkins*

203. Who invented the railway signal?

    a - *Garrett A. Morgan*
    b - *A. B. Blackburn*
    c - *Henry Blair*

204. Who nursed thousands of sick and wounded soldiers and former slaves during the Civil War?

    a - *Sojourner Truth*
    b - *Harriet Tubman*
    c - *Phyllis Wheatley*

205. Who was the first African American to head the Centers for Disease Control?

    a - *David Satcher*
    b - *Charles Drew*
    c - *Joycelyn Elders*

206. G. F. Grant received a patent in 1899 for what sports item?

    a - *Basketball hoop*
    b - *Golf tee*
    c - *Roller skate*

207. In 1953, Solomon Harper invented what thermostatically controlled device?

    a - *Electric blanket*
    b - *Car heater*
    c - *Hair curlers*

208. Whose concept of a movable school, with teachers and equipment traveling to remote areas to instruct the poor in agriculture and nutrition, was later adopted in underdeveloped areas around the world?

    a - *Harriet Tubman*
    b - *George Washington Carver*
    c - *Ernest Everett Just*

209. What did George Washington Carver use to develop shaving cream, paper, ink, rubbing oil, synthetic rubber, and instant coffee?

    a - *Sweet potatoes*
    b - *Soybeans*
    c - *Peanuts*

210. What African American inventor received patents for the lawn mower and the venetian blind restringer?

    a - *Clarence Nokes*
    b - *Paul Williams*
    c - *Norbert Rillieux*

211. What did George Washington Carver use to develop postage stamp glue?

    a - *Peanuts*
    b - *Sweet potatoes*
    c - *Soybeans*

212. Who discovered a soybean oil extract that gave relief to arthritis sufferers?

    a - *Percy Julian*
    b - *Charles Drew*
    c - *George Washington Carver*

213. Albert Y. Garner received a patent for an invention that is used to help save lives. He developed:

    a - *An air bag*
    b - *A ventilator*
    c - *A flame retardant*

214. Who really built the first model steam engine but was unable to patent his work because he was a slave?

    a - *Jan Matzeliger*
    b - *Elijah McCoy*
    c - *Benjamin Bradley*

215. Who patented a means of propulsion for airplanes in 1920?

    a - *James Adams*
    b - *Jan Matzeliger*
    c - *James Forten, Sr.*

216. Who patented a coin-changing machine in 1970?

    a - *James Bauer*
    b - *Donald Jefferson*
    c - *Vincent Gill*

217. Who invented the gas mask?

    a - *Louis Wright*
    b - *Garrett A. Morgan*
    c - *Lewis Latimer*

A legendary frontiersman, James Beckwourth traveled the West, fur-trapping, establishing general stores, living with Indian tribes, and discovering what became known as the Beckwourth Pass to California.

218. Who invented the disposable syringe?

> **a** - *Lloyd Hall*
> **b** - *Elijah McCoy*
> **c** - *Phil Brooks*

219. Who patented a home security system?

> **a** - *Marie Brown*
> **b** - *Frederick McKinley Jones*
> **c** - *Asa Taylor*

220. What spacecraft exploded shortly after liftoff, killing Ronald McNair and the other astronauts on board?

> **a** - *Discovery*
> **b** - *Columbia*
> **c** - *Challenger*

221. What African American inventor patented the cotton planter and the seed planter?

> **a** - *George Washington Carver*
> **b** - *Henry Blair*
> **c** - *Elijah McCoy*

222. What African American inventor patented the hearing aid?

    a - *Harry Hopkins*
    b - *Donald Cotton*
    c - *Vincent Gill*

223. Who became the first African American U.S. surgeon general?

    a - *Percy Julian*
    b - *Louis Wright*
    c - *Joycelyn Elders*

224. Who invented the automatic car washer?

    a - *Jan Matzeliger*
    b - *Richard Spike*
    c - *R. F. Fleming*

225. What African American invented the railway telegraph?

    a - *Granville T. Woods*
    b - *W. B. Purvis*
    c - *Andrew Beard*

226. What African American inventor received a patent for the guitar?

    a - *Granville T. Woods*
    b - *R. F. Fleming*
    c - *Jan Matzeliger*

227. What African American invented the air brake?

    a - *Lewis Latimer*
    b - *Granville T. Woods*
    c - *Elijah McCoy*

228. Theodore K. Lawless was recognized as one of the world's leading:

    a - *Dermatologists*
    b - *Cardiologists*
    c - *Gynecologists*

229. Who was credited with setting up the first blood banks in England and the United States?

    a - *Charles Drew*
    b - *Percy Julian*
    c - *Lloyd Hall*

230. Who launched a campaign in 1947 to open membership to blacks in the American Medical Association?

    a - *Louis Wright*
    b - *Percy Julian*
    c - *Charles Drew*

231. What useful household tool did L. D. Newman receive a patent for in 1898?

    a - *Scouring pad*
    b - *Brush*
    c - *Kitchen knife*

232. Harry C. Hopkins received a patent for enhancing what medical device?

    a - *Pacemaker*
    b - *Hearing aid*
    c - *Artificial limb*

233. James Huntley received a patent for what life-saving mechanism?

    a - *Emergency fire escape*
    b - *Auto air bag*
    c - *Heart defibrillator*

234. Donald E. Jefferson invented what mechanism used by construction crews?

    a - *Earth mover*
    b - *Wrecking ball*
    c - *Triggered exploding wire device*

235. Darnley Howard, Sr., and Darnley Howard, Jr., father and son, shared what profession?

    a - *Explorers*
    b - *Biologists*
    c - *Inventors*

236. In 1927, what African American scientist and inventor received a patent for his process of producing paint?

    a - *Lewis Latimer*
    b - *George Washington Carver*
    c - *L. D. Newman*

George Washington Carver devoted his life to solving the problems faced by southern farmers, pioneering studies of crop disease, experimenting with inexpensive ways to renew soil, and developing 325 uses for peanut crops.

237. Who invented a method for growing oxide?

    a - *Cortland Dugger*
    b - *James Beckwourth*
    c - *W. B. Purvis*

238. What African American inventor received a patent in 1970 for a urinalysis machine?

    a - *Sarah Boone*
    b - *Percy Julian*
    c - *Dewey Sanderson*

239. In 1973, who became the first African American woman to earn a Ph.D. from the prestigious Massachusetts Institute of Technology (MIT)?

    a - *Shirley Ann Jackson*
    b - *Joycelyn Elders*
    c - *Marian Wright Edelman*

240. What African American inventor received a patent for an airplane safety device in 1921?

    a - *Charles Drew*
    b - *Hubert Julian*
    c - *Ralph Bunche*

241. What African American invented an exhaust purifier?

    a - *Rufus Stokes*
    b - *Charles Chesnutt*
    c - *William Hastie*

242. (True or False) Elijah McCoy invented an automatic lubrication system in 1872.

243. What famous scientist and biologist said, "God gave them to me, why should I claim to own them," with regard to his discoveries and inventions?

    a - *Ernest Everett Just*
    b - *George Washington Carver*
    c - *Charles Drew*

244. What outspoken advocate for public health issues was the first woman and the first African American to become president of Planned Parenthood?

    a - *Faye Wattleton*
    b - *Marian Wright Edelman*
    c - *Maya Angelou*

245. What African American cowboy invented bulldogging?

    a - *Matthew Henson*
    b - *James Beckwourth*
    c - *Bill Pickett*

246. Who invented the riding saddle for horses?

    a - *Bill Pickett*
    b - *W. D. Davis*
    c - *Alain Locke*

247. In 1890, W. B. Purvis patented what mechanism used to help communicate information?

    a - *Telegraph*
    b - *Fountain pen*
    c - *Pencil*

248. What African American invented an inexpensive method of refining sugar?

    a - *Norbert Rillieux*
    b - *George Washington Carver*
    c - *Benjamin Banneker*

249. Granville T. Woods, known as the "Black Edison," has how many inventions to his credit?

    a - *23*
    b - *41*
    c - *Over 50*

250. What famous inventor worked as a machinist, blacksmith, railroad fireman, and railroad engineer?

    a - *Benjamin Banneker*
    b - *Frederick McKinley Jones*
    c - *Granville T. Woods*

251. What device used by firefighters was invented by Garrett A. Morgan?

    a - *Power water hose*
    b - *Breathing device*
    c - *Fireproof clothing*

252. (True or False) Andrew Beard invented the lawn sprinkler.

253. What common saying refers to a famous African American inventor?

    a - *"Blood is thicker than water"*
    b - *"Is it the real McCoy?"*
    c - *"Science is the mother of invention"*

254. Who taught himself French and German in order to instruct foreign workers installing electric lights?

    a - *Garrett A. Morgan*
    b - *Lewis Latimer*
    c - *Ernest Everett Just*

255. (True or False) The automatic gearshift was invented by Granville T. Woods.

256. L. F. Brown invented what device for horses?

    a - *Bridle bit*
    b - *Blinders*
    c - *Horseshoes*

257. The oil lubricating cup was invented by what African American?

    a - *Elijah McCoy*
    b - *Frederick McKinley Jones*
    c - *Charles Drew*

258. What landscaping tool did Elijah McCoy patent?

    a - *Lawn mower*
    b - *Weed trimmer*
    c - *Lawn sprinkler*

259. What African American is a respected physicist with more than 100 published scientific articles and abstracts?

    a - *Guion Bluford, Jr.*
    b - *Shirley Ann Jackson*
    c - *Mae Jemison*

260. A. Miles patented what mechanical device used in most office buildings and skyscrapers?

    a - *Automatic window washers*
    b - *Elevator*
    c - *Emergency lights*

261. George Washington Carver revolutionized the agricultural industry with his methods for extracting products from peanuts, sweet potatoes, and:

    a - *Soybeans*
    b - *Rice*
    c - *Onions*

262. Who began doing most of his research at the Sorbonne in Paris to escape American racial prejudice?

    a - *Benjamin Banneker*
    b - *Ernest Everett Just*
    c - *Lewis Latimer*

263. What item used by professional sports teams and the military was patented by Frederick McKinley Jones?

    a - *Helmets*
    b - *Portable X-ray machine*
    c - *Mouthpiece*

264. What African American inventor worked for both General Electric and Westinghouse?

    a - *Lewis Latimer*
    b - *Granville T. Woods*
    c - *Charles Drew*

265. Who received a patent for his invention of a mass-release mechanism for satellites?

    a - *Benjamin Banneker*
    b - *Charles Drew*
    c - *Wilson Hull*

266. Who received a patent for an airplane safety device?

    a - *Hubert Julian*
    b - *Ronald McNair*
    c - *Granville T. Woods*

267. What African American patented a mechanical potato digger?

    a - *George Washington Carver*
    b - *P. D. Smith*
    c - *Norbert Rillieux*

268. Who invented directional signals for the automobile?

    a - *Garrett A. Morgan*
    b - *Granville T. Woods*
    c - *Richard Spike*

269. Who convinced doctors to use blood plasma for transfusions?

    a - *Charles Drew*
    b - *Rebecca Cole*
    c - *Daniel Hale Williams*

270. Guion Bluford, Jr., became the first African American in space aboard the *Challenger* space shuttle. Approximately how much did the space shuttle weigh?

    a - *25 tons*
    b - *50 tons*
    c - *100 tons*

The first African American to work toward the advanced degree of doctor of science in medicine, Charles Drew was an accomplished surgeon and educator who performed ground-breaking research on blood plasma.

271. When Guion Bluford, Jr., orbited earth aboard the *Challenger* space shuttle, how fast did the spacecraft move?

    a - *100 miles per minute*
    b - *300 miles per minute*
    c - *300 miles per hour*

272. What black scientist's grandfather claimed to have been a prince in Africa?

    a - *George Washington Carver*
    b - *Benjamin Banneker*
    c - *Ernest Everett Just*

273. Who earned a reputation for manufacturing soya products, pharmaceuticals, and hormones?

    a - *George Washington Carver*
    b - *Charles Drew*
    c - *Percy Julian*

274. (True or False) Percy Julian made important breakthroughs in the study of human reproduction.

275. In 1901, Garrett Morgan sold his first invention, a belt fastener for sewing machines, for how much money?

    a - *$5*
    b - *$50*
    c - *$2,000*

276. What famous sports figure received a patent on an improved monkey wrench?

    a - *Joe Louis*
    b - *Jack Johnson*
    c - *Muhammad Ali*

277. Who revolutionized the baking industry with the invention of a dough roller?

    a - *Benjamin Banneker*
    b - *Booker T. Washington*
    c - *J. W. Reed*

278. (True or False) Granville T. Woods invented the electric arc lamp.

279. (True or False) George Washington Carver is credited with 25 electrical inventions.

280. Dr. William Hinton is credited with creating a test to detect what disease?

    a - *Alzheimer's disease*
    b - *Cancer*
    c - *Syphilis*

281. Who became a millionaire from developing and selling hair products and designing the hotcomb for black hair?

    a - *Solomon Harper*
    b - *Mary McLeod Bethune*
    c - *Madam C. J. Walker*

282. What frontier explorer became a wealthy businessman, owning a large home, a stable, a barn, a smokehouse, a workshop, a dairy, and a trading post?

    a - *James Beckwourth*
    b - *Jean DuSable*
    c - *Bill Pickett*

283. What famous explorer paddled over 600 miles up the Mississippi River?

  a - *Jean DuSable*
  b - *Matthew Henson*
  c - *Barney Ford*

284. What organization of African Americans sought to explore and settle in Africa?

  a - *National Association for the Advancement of Colored People*
  b - *American Colonization Society*
  c - *Beckwourth Explorers Society*

285. What was the name of the first science book written by an African American scientist?

  a - *Principles of Science*
  b - *Almanack*
  c - *Science Doctorates*

286. What explorer departed for a famous expedition aboard the ship *Roosevelt* on July 6, 1908?

  a - *Jean DuSable*
  b - *Matthew Henson*
  c - *Frederick Gregory*

287. Who was the first African American member of the National Academy of Sciences?

  a - *Professor Nathan Irvin Huggins*
  b - *Professor David H. Blackwell*
  c - *George Washington Carver*

288. Who was the first African American member of the U.S. Atomic Energy Commission?

  a - *Granville T. Woods*
  b - *Guion Bluford, Jr.*
  c - *Samuel Nabrit*

289. In what year did Matthew Henson reach the North Pole?

  a - *1880*
  b - *1909*
  c - *1929*

A tireless explorer, Matthew Henson played a crucial role in most of Admiral Robert Peary's famous expeditions, breaking the trail to become the first man to reach the North Pole.

290. Matthew Henson learned the language and skills of what Indian tribe?

    a - *The Inuit*
    b - *The Mohawk*
    c - *The Crow*

291. In 1822, African American pioneers founded what colony on the west coast of Africa?

    a - *Ghana*
    b - *Guyana*
    c - *Liberia*

292. What African American was the first to explore the longest cave in the world, Mammoth Cave in Kentucky?

    a - *Matthew Henson*
    b - *Stephen Bishop*
    c - *James Beckwourth*

293. What black explorer became the first settler on Puget Sound?

    a - *Jean DuSable*
    b - *Barney Ford*
    c - *George W. Bush*

294. Who was known as "Stagecoach Mary" and was the first African American woman to drive a U.S. mail coach?

    a - *Ma Rainey*
    b - *Mary Fields*
    c - *Mary Beckwourth*

295. How many years did Matthew Henson and his group search for the North Pole?

    a - *10*
    b - *18*
    c - *31*

296. Who came from Haiti, spoke French, and explored the Great Lakes area?

    a - *Toussaint L'Ouverture*
    b - *George W. Bush*
    c - *Jean DuSable*

297. In 1908, who founded an African American town in California where blacks could run their own businesses and government?

    a - *Allen Allensworth*
    b - *Jean DuSable*
    c - *James Beckwourth*

298. (True or False) The "Beckwourth Pass" opened a route to West Virginia.

299. James Beckwourth befriended what Native American tribe?

    a - *The Iroquois*
    b - *The Crow*
    c - *The Seminole*

300. Who wrote *The Negro Trailblazers of California,* the first record of many black pioneers' contributions?

    a - *James Beckwourth*
    b - *Delilah Beasley*
    c - *James Fenimore Cooper*

301. When James Beckwourth became a warrior for a Native American tribe what nickname did he earn?

    a - *Wild Sun*
    b - *Bloody Arm*
    c - *Crazy Jim*

302. (True or False) Mae Jemison was the first African American woman to travel in space.

303. (True or False) James Beckwourth became a chief of the Crow Nation and was called "Chief Medicine Calf."

304. Who led the first wagon train through the Sierra Nevada into Northern California?

    a - *Allen Allensworth*
    b - *Jean DuSable*
    c - *James Beckwourth*

305. What did Benjamin Banneker's book, *Almanack,* examine?

    a - *The human body*
    b - *Chemical reactions*
    c - *The sun, moon, and planets*

306. Who was the first African American to pilot a space shuttle mission?

    a - *Guion Bluford, Jr.*
    b - *Ronald McNair*
    c - *Frederick Gregory*

307. What daring aviator became the first African American woman to have an international pilot's license?

    a - *Bessie Coleman*
    b - *Mae Jemison*
    c - *Faye Wattleton*

308. What person on the *Challenger* space shuttle was President Ronald Reagan speaking to when he said, "You are paving the way for others"?

    a - *Ronald McNair*
    b - *Guion Bluford, Jr.*
    c - *Frederick Gregory*

309. What was special about the first space shuttle flight flown by Guion Bluford, Jr.?

    a - *First U.S. space shuttle mission*
    b - *First shuttle launch at night*
    c - *First reusable spaceship*

310. Who carried some small West African art objects on a space mission to show that space belongs to all countries?

    a - *Mae Jemison*
    b - *Ronald McNair*
    c - *Frederick Gregory*

311. What caused the disaster of the *Challenger* space shuttle, which led to the death of astronaut Ronald McNair and others?

    a - *Midair collision*
    b - *Computer malfunction*
    c - *Faulty "O" rings*

312. (True or False) Edward A. Bouchet earned a Ph.D. in physics from Yale University in 1876, becoming the first African American to receive a doctorate degree.

313. Which of the following items was not carried by frontier explorer James Beckwourth?

    a - *Rifle*
    b - *Knife*
    c - *Map*

314. What did Thomas A. Jennings, one of the first African Americans to receive a patent, invent in 1821?

    a - *Container to preserve food*
    b - *Dry scouring device for clothing*
    c - *Heating element for cooking*

315. What measuring instrument was invented by Frederick McKinley Jones?

    a - *Barometer*
    b - *Altimeter*
    c - *Thermostat*

316. Warren M. Washington, the first African American elected president of the American Meteorological Society, founded the Black Environmental Science Trust:

    a - *To find a solution to the hole in the ozone layer*
    b - *To draw attention to the environmental problems faced by minorities, such as increased exposure to lead and pollution*
    c - *To study the climate and environment of Africa*

317. (True or False) Daniel Hale Williams founded Provident Hospital in Chicago, the first hospital in the country with an interracial staff.

318. Who worked for Samuel Morse, the inventor of the telegraph, and later became the first African American museum assistant at the Smithsonian Institution?

    a - *Garrett A. Morgan*
    b - *Granville T. Woods*
    c - *Solomon G. Brown*

319. Marjorie Stewart Joyner patented a:

    a - *Washing machine*
    b - *Sewing machine*
    c - *Permanent wave machine*

320. (True or False) Elijah McCoy was responsible for more than 20 lubrication inventions.

321. (True or False) Alexander Graham Bell invited George Washington Carver to join him in Orange, New Jersey, as an associate.

322. Who became the first and only black doctor to treat a U.S. president when he cared for President James A. Garfield's wounds from an assassin's bullet?

    a - *Daniel Hale Williams*
    b - *Charles Burleigh Purvis*
    c - *Charles Drew*

323. In 1885, who received a patent for a "folding cabinet bed," a predecessor of the convertible sofa?

    a - *Ida Gray*
    b - *Sarah Goode*
    c - *Lewis Temple*

324. Who invented the first corn harvester?

    a - *Elijah McCoy*
    b - *Percy Julian*
    c - *Henry Blair*

325. The first national monument dedicated to an African American honors which revered scientist?

    a - *Lewis Latimer*
    b - *George Washington Carver*
    c - *Ronald McNair*

ANSWERS

1. a **Madam C. J. Walker**
2. a **Dr. Roland Scott**
3. b **Beckwourth Pass**
4. a **Dr. Harold Fleming**
5. a **Clothes dryer**
6. a **Dr. Daniel Hale Williams**
7. a **Jan E. Matzeliger**
8. a **Los Angeles**
9. a **James Derham**
10. a **J. T. Winters**
11. a **Guion S. Bluford, Jr.**
12. a **L. J. Love**
13. a **Conversion of gas into electricity**
14. a **W. B. Purvis**
15. c **Peanuts**
16. a **Susan McKinney**
17. b **Granville T. Woods**
18. **False - Electric lamp**
19. c **Ronald McNair**
20. **True**
21. **True**
22. c **Range**
23. b **T. W. Stewart**
24. b **George E. Carruthers**
25. b **F. A. Hilyer**
26. b **Project physician**
27. b **L. C. Bailey**
28. a **Joseph L. Parker**
29. a **Jet propulsion balloon**
30. b **Wendell Belfield**
31. a **Andrew Beard**
32. a **Dorothy McClendon**
33. b **Solomon Harper**
34. b **Waste management system**
35. c **Percy Julian**

36. c **James Forten, Sr.**
37. c **Matthew Henson**
38. b **Sarah Boone**
39. b **Delano Meriwether**
40. b **Cortisone**
41. b **Sojourner Truth**
42.   **False - Francis Butler**
43.   **True**
44. b ***Apollo***
45. b **Dr. William Hinton**
46. b **1960s**
47. b **Theodore K. Lawless**
48. b **Garrett A. Morgan**
49. c **Exhaust purification system**
50. b **Dr. Levi Watkins, Jr.**
51. b **Henry Blair**
52. b **Charles Turner**
53. b **J. T. Marshall**
54. a **Ozzie Williams**
55. b **Dr. Louis Wright**
56. c **Emmanual L. Logan**
57. b **Archie Alexander**
58. b **W. D. Davis**
59. c **Benjamin Banneker**
60. a **George Washington Carver**
61.   **True**
62. c **Dr. Louis T. Wright**
63. c **Incandescent electric light**
64. a **Frederick McKinley Jones**
65. a **Andrew J. Beard**
66. c **Physician**
67. a **James Beckwourth**
68. c **York**
69.   **True**
70. c **Lewis Howard Latimer**
71. a **Telegraph system between moving trains**
72. c **Carbon filament in incandescent electric lights**
73. c **Jenny coupler**
74.   **True**
75. c **Soybean chemist**
76.   **False - Gas mask**
77.   **True**
78. a **Joseph Lee**
79. a **Blacksmith**
80.   **False - Andrew J. Beard**
81.   **True**
82.   **True**
83. a **James Forten, Sr.**
84. a **Granville T. Woods**

85.   False - Chicago, Illinois
86. b Jefferson Davis
87. c Meharry Medical College
88. a James Beckwourth
89. b Because he stole horses from white men
90. b Benjamin Banneker
91. c Twelve
92. a Diamond Grove, Missouri
93.   True
94. c 1943
95. a Tennessee
96. b 1876
97. a Eschikagou
98.   False - American Heart Association
99. a James Beckwourth
100. b New Orleans, Louisiana
101. a Open-heart surgery
102. b Rotary engine
103. c Fertilizer distributor
104. a Marine eggs
105.   True
106. a Matthew Henson
107. b D. E. Howard
108. c Henry T. Blair
109. b Arizona and New Mexico
110.   False - Co-discoverer of the North Pole
111. b Admiral Robert E. Peary
112. c Guion Bluford, Jr.
113. a Elijah McCoy
114. b Granville T. Woods
115. a Garrett A. Morgan
116. a Ernest Everett Just
117. b Dolphus Milligan
118. a Matthew Henson
119. c Charles Brooks
120. c Benjamin Banneker
121. b Dr. Roland Scott
122. c Bruce Lee
123. b Mary Elizabeth Mahoney
124.   True
125. b J. W. Smith
126. b Charles Beckley
127. b Dr. Samuel L. Koontz
128. b J. A. Burr
129. a E. G. Becket
130. a Mary Middleton
131. b Louis Alexander
132. a Benjamin Banneker
133. c Otis Boykin

134. b F.W. Leslie
135. b Dr. Carrol M. Leevy
136. a J. Standard
137. a Dr. Charles Drew
138. a Dr. Percy Julian
139. a James Parsons
140.   False - Astronaut
141. b R. B. Spike
142. b L. P. Ray
143. b Booker T. Hoagan
144. a Garrett A. Morgan
145. c Charles Spurgeon Fletcher
146. a Frederick McKinley Jones
147. b A. W. Martin
148. a William Hinton
149. a John Coleman
150. c Dr. Jane C. Wright
151. b Ernest Everett Just
152.   True
153. a Dr. Mae Jemison
154. c 1983
155. a Meredith Gourdine
156. b Onesimus
157. a Lewis Latimer
158. b George Washington Carver
159.   False - Booker T. Washington
160. a Chicago's Provident Hospital
161.   True
162.   False - Dr. Louis Wright
163. a 1923
164. c 20
165. a Physician
166. c Throat
167. b Astronaut
168. b Charles Drew
169. a Frederick McKinley Jones
170.   True
171. b Black medical association
172.   True
173. a A. Miles
174. c Jan Matzeliger
175. c W. Lincoln Hawkins
176. a 1890
177. b Percy Julian
178. a Dr. Percy Julian
179.   True
180. a Benjamin Banneker
181. a Joe Anderson
182. c 1968

183. c **Sail control for ships**
184. a **Ernest Everett Just**
185. a **Lewis Latimer**
186. b **J. Standard**
187. b **Madam C. J. Walker**
188. a **Jamaica Train**
189.   **False - He won for agricultural chemistry research**
190. a **Mary Mahoney**
191. b **James O. Plinton, Jr.**
192. c **Modified airship**
193. b **Slave labor**
194. a **T. J. Boyd**
195. a **Tuskegee Institute, Alabama**
196. c **$40,000**
197. b **Dr. Ernest Everett Just**
198. c **Both a and b**
199. b **All-black cavalry**
200. a **Develop atomic power**
201. b **George Washington Carver**
202. b **L. Douglas Wilder**
203. b **A. B. Blackburn**
204. b **Harriet Tubman**
205. a **David Satcher**
206. b **Golf tee**
207. c **Hair curlers**
208. b **George Washington Carver**
209. c **Peanuts**
210. a **Clarence Nokes**
211. b **Sweet potatoes**
212. a **Percy Julian**
213. c **A flame retardant**
214. c **Benjamin Bradley**
215. a **James Adams**
216. a **James Bauer**
217. b **Garrett A. Morgan**
218. c **Phil Brooks**
219. a **Marie Brown**
220. c ***Challenger***
221. b **Henry Blair**
222. a **Harry Hopkins**
223. c **Joycelyn Elders**
224. b **Richard Spike**
225. a **Granville T. Woods**
226. b **R. F. Fleming**
227. b **Granville T. Woods**
228. a **Dermatologists**
229. a **Charles Drew**
230. c **Charles Drew**
231. b **Brush**

232. b **Hearing aid**
233. a **Emergency fire escape**
234. c **Triggered exploding wire device**
235. c **Inventors**
236. b **George Washington Carver**
237. a **Cortland Dugger**
238. c **Dewey Sanderson**
239. a **Shirley Ann Jackson**
240. b **Hubert Julian**
241. a **Rufus Stokes**
242.   **True**
243. b **George Washington Carver**
244. a **Faye Wattleton**
245. c **Bill Pickett**
246. b **W. D. Davis**
247. b **Fountain pen**
248. a **Norbert Rillieux**
249. c **Over 50**
250. c **Granville T. Woods**
251. b **Breathing device**
252.   **False - He invented a railroad car coupling device**
253. b **"Is it the real McCoy?"**
254. b **Lewis Latimer**
255.   **False - It was invented by Richard Spike**
256. a **Bridle bit**
257. a **Elijah McCoy**
258. c **Lawn sprinkler**
259. b **Shirley Ann Jackson**
260. b **Elevator**
261. a **Soybeans**
262. b **Ernest Everett Just**
263. b **Portable X-ray machine**
264. a **Lewis Latimer**
265. c **Wilson Hull**
266. a **Hubert Julian**
267. b **P. D. Smith**
268. c **Richard Spike**
269. a **Charles Drew**
270. c **100 tons**
271. b **300 miles per minute**
272. b **Benjamin Banneker**
273. c **Percy Julian**
274.   **True**
275. b **$50.00**
276. b **Jack Johnson**
277. c **J. W. Reed**
278.   **False - Lewis Latimer**
279.   **False - Granville T. Woods**

280. c **Syphilis**
281. c **Madam C. J. Walker**
282. b **Jean DuSable**
283. a **Jean DuSable**
284. b **American Colonization Society**
285. b ***Almanack***
286. b **Matthew Henson**
287. b **Professor David H. Blackwell**
288. c **Samuel Nabrit**
289. b **1909**
290. a **The Inuit**
291. c **Liberia**
292. b **Stephen Bishop**
293. c **George W. Bush**
294. b **Mary Fields**
295. b **18**
296. c **Jean DuSable**
297. a **Allen Allensworth**
298.   **False - California**
299. b **The Crow**
300. b **Delilah Beasley**
301. b **Bloody Arm**
302.   **True**
303.   **True**
304. c **James Beckwourth**
305. c **The sun, moon, and planets**
306. c **Frederick Gregory**
307. a **Bessie Coleman**
308. b **Guion Bluford, Jr.**
309. b **First shuttle launch at night**
310. a **Mae Jemison**
311. c **Faulty "O" rings**
312.   **True**
313. c **Map**
314. b **Dry scouring device for clothing**
315. c **Thermostat**
316. b **To draw attention to the environmental problems faced by minorities, such as increased exposure to lead and pollution**
317.   **True**
318. c **Solomon G. Brown**
319. c **Permanent wave machine**
320.   **True**
321.   **False - Thomas Edison invited George Washington Carver to join him**
322. b **Charles Burleigh Purvis**
323. b **Sarah Goode**
324. c **Henry Blair**
325. b **George Washington Carver**

INDEX

R. S. RENNERT has edited the nearly 100 volumes in Chelsea House's award-winning BLACK AMERICANS OF ACHIEVEMENT series, which tells the stories of black men and women who have helped shape the course of modern history, and the 10 volumes in the PROFILES OF GREAT BLACK AMERICANS series. He is also the author of several sports biographies, including *Henry Aaron, Jesse Owens,* and *Jackie Robinson.*